JOHN CORIGLIANO
SNAPSHOT: CIRCA 1909
for String Quartet

*"Snapshot: Circa 1909" was commissioned by the Elements String Quartet
which presented its World Premiere November 18, 2003
at Merkin Concert Hall, New York City.*

*"Snapshot: Circa 1909" has been recorded
by the Corigliano Quartet
for NAXOS.*

duration ca. 6 minutes

ED 4255
First Printing: May 2005

ISBN 1-423-40033-x

G. SCHIRMER, Inc.

DISTRIBUTED BY

HAL•LEONARD®
CORPORATION

7777 W. BLUEMOUND RD. P.O. BOX 13819 MILWAUKEE, WI 53213

When the Elements Quartet asked me to write a piece inspired by a photograph, I immediately thought of one I have had since I was a child. It was taken in Greenwich Village in my grandparents' Sullivan Street apartment, which I have only seen in photos.

The photographer came to do a group shot of my grandparents, whom I never met, and their six children. After taking that picture, the photographer was coaxed into doing a shot of my father and his brother Peter performing on violin and guitar.

The picture has never ceased to move me. My father looked about eight years old, wearing knickers and earnestly bowing his violin, while my uncle, then a teenager, held a guitar in an aristocratic position and stared at the camera.

In the short quartet inspired by the photo, the second violin plays a nostalgic melody, while the other strings pluck their instruments in a guitar-like manner. This solo is obviously the boy violinist singing through his instrument.

After the melody is completed, however, the first violin enters, muted, in the very highest register. In my mind, he was playing the dream that my eight-year-old father must have had -- of performing roulades and high, virtuosic, musing passages that were still impossible for him to master.

This young violinist grew into a great soloist -- my father, John Corigliano, concertmaster of the New York Philharmonic for over a quarter century. He, as an adult, performed the concerti and solos that as a child he could only imagine.

The two violins, boy and dream, join together at the end as the guitar sounds play on.

John Corigliano

The photograph on the front cover is available for download from Mr. Corigliano's biography page at www.schirmer.com

for Jeffrey Multer

SNAPSHOT: CIRCA 1909
for String Quartet

John Corigliano

* Either Vn. I or Vlc. should play this C#

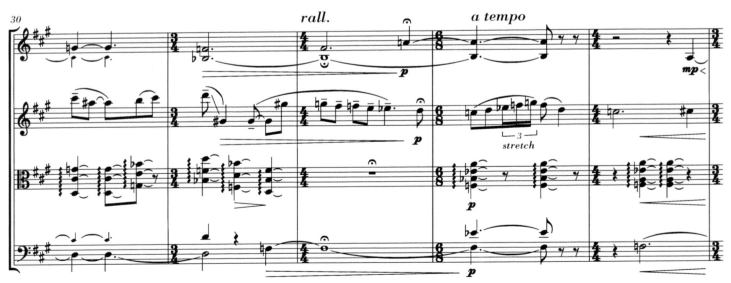

* Either Vn. I or Vlc. should play this C#

JOHN CORIGLIANO
SNAPSHOT: CIRCA 1909
for String Quartet

Violin I

ED 4255
First Printing: May 2005

ISBN 1-423-40033-x

G. SCHIRMER, *Inc.*

DISTRIBUTED BY

7777 W. BLUEMOUND RD. P.O. BOX 13819 MILWAUKEE, WI 53213

Violin I

for Jeffrey Multer

SNAPSHOT: CIRCA 1909
for String Quartet

John Corigliano

* Either Vn. I or Vlc. should play this C#

G. SCHIRMER, Inc.

DISTRIBUTED BY

JOHN CORIGLIANO
SNAPSHOT: CIRCA 1909
for String Quartet

Violin II

ED 4255
First Printing: May 2005

ISBN 1-423-40033-x

G. SCHIRMER, *Inc.*

DISTRIBUTED BY

HAL•LEONARD®
CORPORATION
7777 W. BLUEMOUND RD. P.O. BOX 13819 MILWAUKEE, WI 53213

Violin II

for Jeffrey Multer

SNAPSHOT: CIRCA 1909
for String Quartet

John Corigliano

G. SCHIRMER, Inc.

DISTRIBUTED BY
HAL•LEONARD®

JOHN CORIGLIANO
SNAPSHOT: CIRCA 1909
for String Quartet

Viola

ED 4255
First Printing: May 2005

ISBN 1-423-40033-x

G. SCHIRMER, Inc.

DISTRIBUTED BY

7777 W. BLUEMOUND RD. P.O. BOX 13819 MILWAUKEE, WI 53213

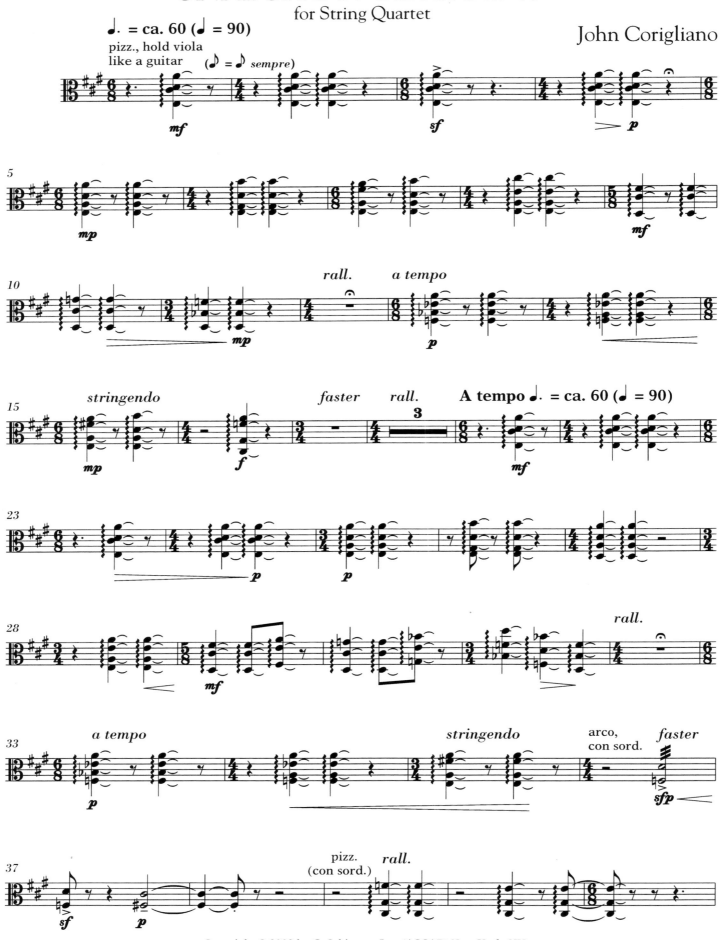

Viola

for Jeffrey Multer

SNAPSHOT: CIRCA 1909
for String Quartet

John Corigliano

G. SCHIRMER, Inc.

DISTRIBUTED BY

JOHN CORIGLIANO
SNAPSHOT: CIRCA 1909
for String Quartet

Violoncello

ED 4255
First Printing: May 2005

ISBN 1-423-40033-x

G. SCHIRMER, Inc.

DISTRIBUTED BY

7777 W. BLUEMOUND RD. P.O. BOX 13819 MILWAUKEE, WI 53213

Violoncello

for Jeffrey Multer
SNAPSHOT: CIRCA 1909
for String Quartet

John Corigliano

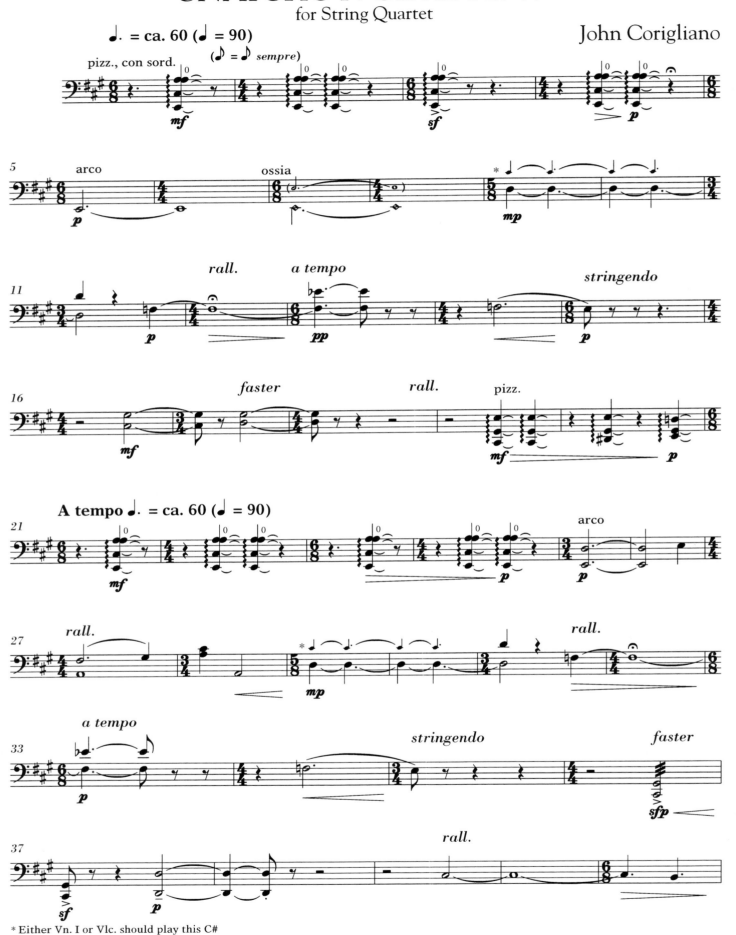

* Either Vn. I or Vlc. should play this C#

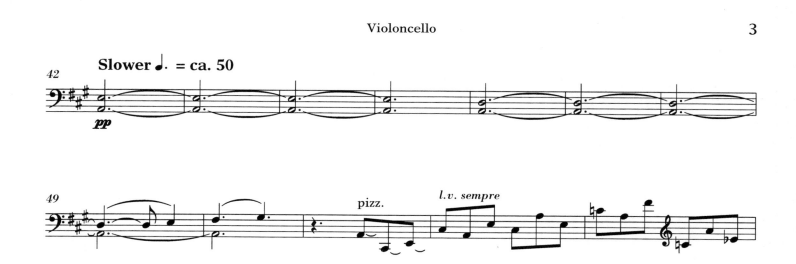

G. SCHIRMER, *Inc.*

DISTRIBUTED BY
HAL•LEONARD®

stringendo   faster   rall.

Slower ♩. = ca. 50

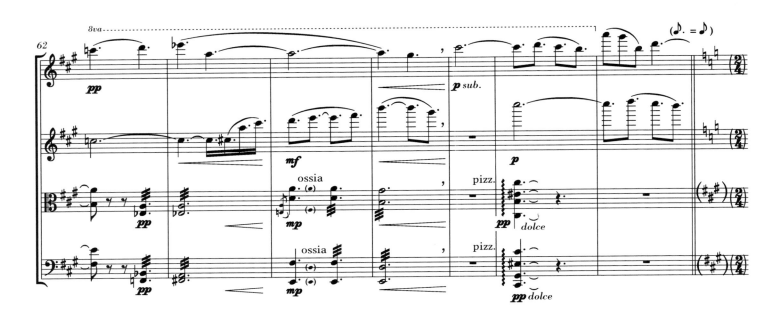

G. SCHIRMER, Inc.

DISTRIBUTED BY
HAL•LEONARD®